For Stardust Children Ollim
& Malachi

Keep on shining!

Joann Rose Leonard

STARDUST CHILD

Joann Rose Leonard
illustrated by
William Schroder

Eifrig Publishing LLC

Berlin   Lemont

Published by Eifrig Publishing,
PO Box 66, Lemont, PA 16851, USA
Knobelsdorffstr. 44,
14059 Berlin, Germany.

For information regarding permission, write to:
Rights and Permissions Department,
Eifrig Publishing,
PO Box 66, Lemont, PA 16851, USA.
permissions@eifrigpublishing.com, +1-888-340-6543

Library of Congress Cataloging-in-Publication Data

 Joann Rose Leonard
Stardust Child by Joann Rose Leonard, illustrated by William Schroder
p. cm.

Paperback: ISBN 978-1-63233-121-2
Hard cover: ISBN 978-1-63233-122-9
Ebook: ISBN 978-1-63233-123-6

[1. Natural Science – Juvenile Fiction. 2. Stars – Juvenile Fiction.]

I. William Schroder ill. II. Title

20 19 18 17 2016
5 4 3 2 1

Printed on FSC certified recycled PCW acid-free paper. ∞

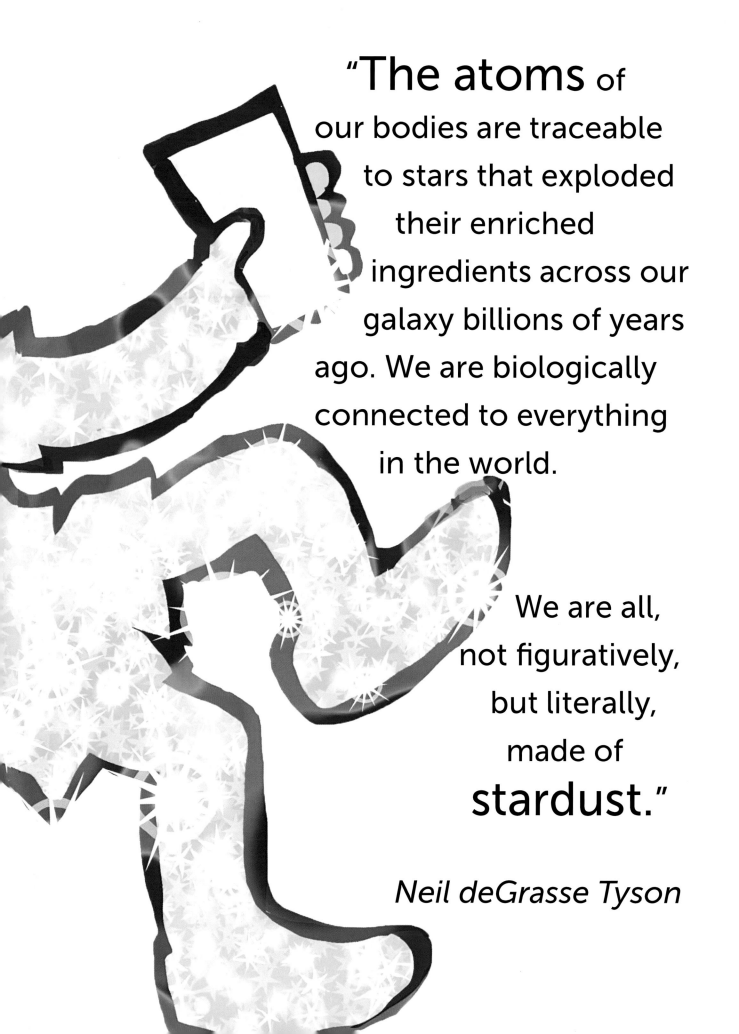

"The atoms of our bodies are traceable to stars that exploded their enriched ingredients across our galaxy billions of years ago. We are biologically connected to everything in the world.

We are all, not figuratively, but literally, made of stardust."

Neil deGrasse Tyson

This is the story of Stardust Chil

4

This is the cow
that makes the milk
that Stardust Child drinks.

This is the farmer
who milks the cow
that makes the milk
that Stardust Child drinks.

This is the grass
the cow eats
to make the milk
that Stardust Child drinks.

These are the burrowing worms
that keep the soil fertile
to feed the grass
the cow eats
to make the milk
that Stardust Child drinks.

This is the sun
that gives light

to grow the grass
the cow eats

to make the milk
that Stardust Child drinks.

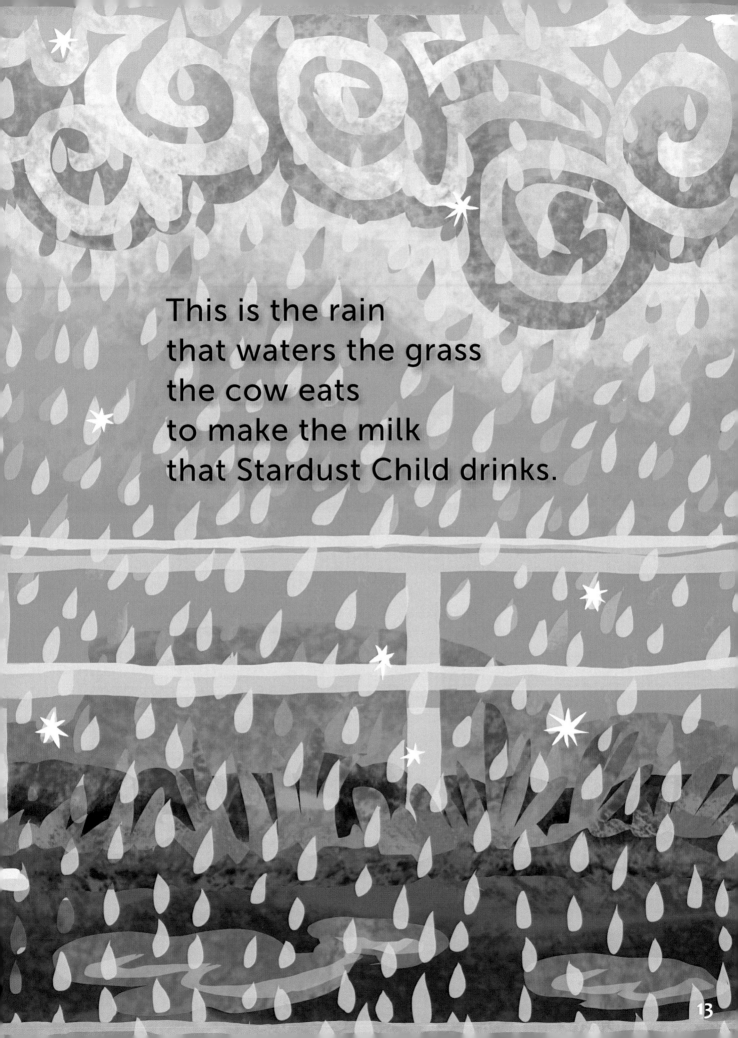

This is the rain
that waters the grass
the cow eats
to make the milk
that Stardust Child drinks.

These are the clouds
that carry the rain
from the sea
to water the grass
the cow eats
to make the milk
that Stardust Child drinks.

These are the whales
and turtles and fish
that swim in the sea
where clouds form

to water the grass
the cow eats
to make the milk
that Stardust Child drinks.

These are the stars
that shine in the night sky
over the sea
where the clouds form
to water the grass
the cow eats

to make the milk
that Stardust Child drinks.

These are the ancient stars

that exploded into stardust

that made the atoms

in the whales
and turtles and fish
that swim in the sea
where the clouds form.

This is the stardust
that made the atoms
in the sun and the soil ...
that grow the grass the cow eats
to make the milk ...
that Stardust Child drinks.

23

And the stardust
that made the atoms

in the cow
that eats the grass
to make the milk
that Stardust Child drinks.

This is the stardust
that made the atoms
of the farmer
who milks the cow
that makes the milk
that Stardust Child drinks.

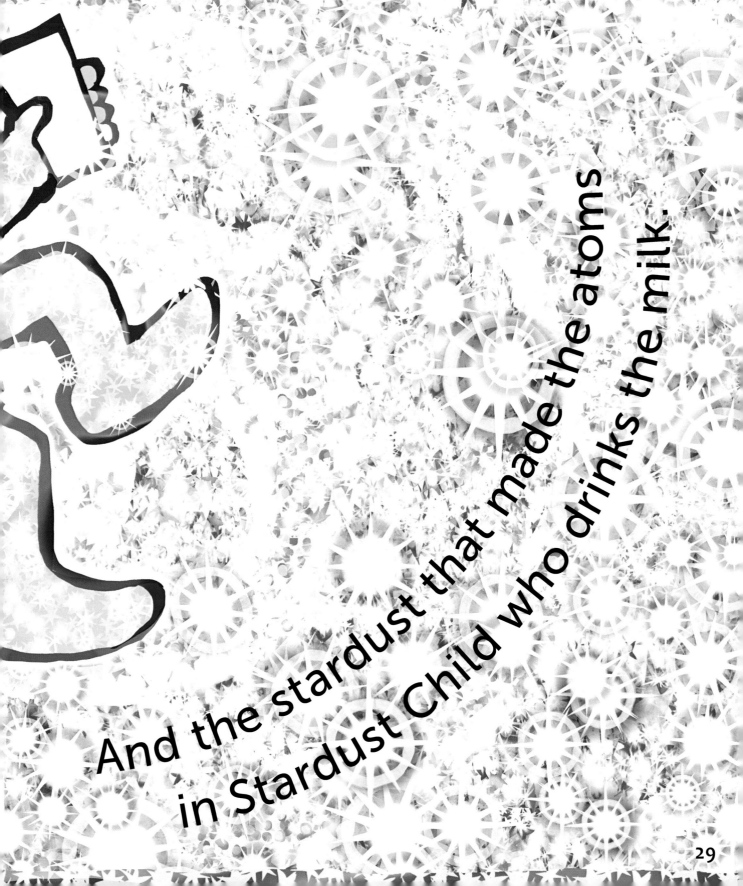

And the stardust that made the atoms
in Stardust Child who drinks the milk.

IN CASE YOU WONDERED...

Everyone — everything — is made of atoms, and all the atoms in the universe came from stars. Think about it — our atoms were in stars before they were in our bodies.

Everything and everyone you see is made of stardust!